John Henry

Adapted by Stephen Krensky
Illustrations by Mark Oldryod

On My Own FOLKLORE

Millbrook Press/Minneapolis

To Dawn, George and Jesse —M.O.

Text copyright © 2007 by Stephen Krensky
Illustrations copyright © 2007 by Lerner Publishing Group, Inc.

Millbrook Press
A division of Lerner Publishing Group, Inc.
241 First Avenue North
Minneapolis, MN 55401 USA

For reading levels and more information, look up this title at www.lernerbooks.com.

Library of Congress Cataloging-in-Publication Data

Krensky, Stephen.
    John Henry / adapted by Stephen Krensky.
       p.   cm. – (On my own folklore)
    Summary: Retells the life of the legendary African American hero who raced against
a steam drill to cut through a mountain.
    ISBN 978–1–57505–887–0 (lib. bdg. : alk. paper)
    ISBN 978–0–8225–7036–3 (EB pdf)
    1. John Henry (Legendary character)—Legends. [1. John Henry (Legendary
character)—Legends. 2. African Americans—Folklore. 3. Tall tales. 4. Folklore—
United States.] I. Title
    PZ8.1.K8663Joh 2007
    398.2'0973'02–dc22   2005010187

Manufactured in the United States of America
5-39471-5419-4/7/2016

John Henry: A Folklore Hero

Maybe you have heard of John Henry. Perhaps someone mentioned his name, or you heard a song about him. Well, John Henry is one of America's tall-tale heroes. Some say John Henry drove steel in West Virginia in the 1800s. Some say he worked in the Deep South. Most agree that he was a real man. And his story became a tall-tale legend.

We call stories like John Henry's tall tales because everything in them is extra big, extra fast, and extra wild. And the truth in these stories might be just a bit stretched. The heroes and heroines in tall tales are as tall as buildings, as strong as oxen, or as fast as lightning. They meet with wild adventures at every turn. But that's okay because they can solve just about every problem that comes their way.

Tall tales may be funny and outsized. But they describe the life that many workers and pioneers shared. The people in these stories often have jobs that real people had. And the stories were always set in familiar places.

The first tellers of these tales may have known these people and places. Or they may have wished they could be just like the hero in the story. The stories were told again and again and passed from person to person. We call such spoken and shared stories folklore.

Folklore is the stories and customs of a place or a people. Folklore can be folktales like the tall tale. These stories are usually not written down until much later, after they have been told and retold for many years. Folklore can also be sayings, jokes, and songs.

Folklore can teach us something. A rhyme or a song may help us remember an event from long ago. Or it can be just for fun, such as a good ghost story or a jump-rope song. Folklore can also tell us about the people who share the stories.

John Henry's tale may have come from the lives of real-life workers. These African American men were born as slaves before the Civil War (1861–1865). They grew up to be free men working for the railroad. Like John Henry, these men helped build America's railways. They succeeded through their own strength—not through the power of machines. Over time, their work was done. And over time, John Henry became a legend.

Getting a Grip

Nobody ever said for sure
that John Henry was born
with a hammer in his hand.
But nobody ever said he wasn't, either.
He always seemed to be holding one.
That was a fact.

While other babies were grabbing
onto fingers and toes,
young John was busy
grabbing hammers.

These weren't big hammers, of course.
They weighed four or five pounds
at most.
John dragged them around behind him,
digging ruts in the dirt.

Then his papa taught him
to walk up and down the cotton fields
in straight lines.
That way, Papa could plant seeds
in the ruts afterward.

By and by, John grew strong enough
to lift his hammer.
The first thing he did
was swing it around.
It was the second thing he did too.
And the third.

Left, right, up, down,
John Henry was not too picky.
He just liked the feel
of the hammer in his hand
and the whooshing sound it made
cutting through the air.

At first, John didn't have much control.
He'd swing the hammer this way
and smash it into a chair.
He'd swing the hammer that way
and break a few dishes.
After a while, his mama made John
swing his hammer outside.

There was a lot more room,
and things weren't so delicate.
Still, all the trees on the Henry farm
had dings and dents.
They showed where young John
had passed by.

One day, John's folks got the notion
of putting his swinging to good use.
They taught John to pound
fence posts into the ground.
John took to the job straightaway.
He started with small picket fences.
Soon he moved on to bigger things.
Up and down the county John went,
planting fence posts
wherever they were needed.

John hardly ever stopped for a rest.
If his right hand needed a break,
he simply shifted to his left.
Sometimes he used both hands
to hit two posts at the same time.
Nobody could match John Henry
once he got rolling.
Folks came from all around to watch him.
He was a wonder, no doubt about it.

Following the Tracks

John Henry liked building fences.
Tall or short,
picket or post,
it made no difference to him.
All he wanted was to stay busy.
Folks could hear John whistling
as he marched to work.
He probably whistled at work too.
But it was hard to be sure.
John's pounding hammer made
so much noise.

Around this time, the railroad began
to cut through the countryside.
The railroad had to be built
track by track.
The railroad company was always looking for
a strong man who could pound a hammer.

It was hard to miss
John Henry.
He stood a head above
most men.
Rocks looked soft
next to the muscles in his arms.

The railroad's foreman was in charge
of the workers.
He had already hired
some powerfully strong men.
One fellow could spit nails into a board
so hard that he didn't need a hammer.
Another worker was so strong
that he bent a rail into a heart
for his favorite gal.

But nobody could match John Henry.
His job was to pound stakes
into the ground or solid rock.
When the stakes were removed,
they left behind holes.
Other workers filled the holes
with explosives.
Each blast blew away part of a hill
or mountain in the railroad's way.

Other men needed four or five whacks
to drive in a stake.
John Henry and his 14-pound hammers
needed only one.

SWISH! went the air
as John's hammers swung down.
CLANG! went the stake
as the hammer drove it home.
The ground shook from the blows
in every direction.
Folks who didn't know better
thought a giant was passing by.

Once John found his rhythm,
his hammer heads glowed burning red.
A few even melted
right off their handles.
When John remembered,
he cooled off his hammers
in a lake or stream.
Sometimes the steam rose so high
people feared a volcano had erupted.

John loved working for the railroad.
He liked seeing the tracks grow
across the countryside.

Each night, he went to sleep
dreaming of the trains to come.
And each morning he awoke,
ready to make that day come
a little sooner.

Big Bend Tunnel

Thanks to John Henry,
the railroad was laying down track
way ahead of schedule.
John was never one to brag, though.
He let the sound of his stakes
do his speaking for him.
Of course, not everyone gave John Henry
credit for doing all the work himself

Some people said the rocks
were afraid of him.
They claimed that the rocks shattered
in nervousness just at the news
John was coming.
John Henry only smiled
when he heard such things.
If he knew better,
he kept it to himself.

But ordinary rocks
were not John Henry's only problem.
Looming in the distance
was Big Bend Mountain.

It was too big to go around.

And it was too steep to go over.

So all the railroad could do

was keep going straight.

That meant digging a tunnel

right through the middle.

Now, Big Bend Mountain wasn't the tallest
mountain anyone had ever seen.
And it wasn't the widest.
But everyone agreed right off
that it was the most ornery mountain
east of the Mississippi River.
The first time someone tried
to pound in a stake,
it snapped in two.

The second time,
the stake crumpled up
like an accordion.
And even when the stakes went in,
they barely made a dent.
It was almost like the mountain
was laughing at them.

More than two years went by,
and still the tunnel wasn't done.
John Henry himself
was clearing 10 to 12 feet a day.
The air was filled with dust and smoke.
It was so hard to see,
the workers never knew
if the sun was shining or not.

On rainy days,

the soot and mud stuck to everyone.

Then men looked like statues come to life.

The work was dangerous too.

Dozens of men were hurt or killed

building the tunnel.

But the men who were left

weren't about to give up.

The Last Contest

One day, a salesman showed up
in the railroad camp.
He looked fancy. He talked fancy.
And he had with him a fancy
steam-powered drill.
Big Bend Mountain was still causing
a whole lot of trouble.

So it was no wonder that
the foreman stopped to listen.
This was no ordinary drill,
the salesman claimed.
It was a truly amazing machine.
It could make the work go faster.
It could outdig any man alive.
Why, a machine like this
was better than 10 men.

John Henry could hardly believe his ears.

He stepped right up to speak.

A machine couldn't be part of a team, he said.

And it took a team to build a railroad.

The salesman had said the machine

could beat ten men.

How about just one?

John would like to see the drill try to beat him!
So the railroad set up a contest
to see who was right.
How many three-foot holes could
John Henry and the drill
make in an hour?
The whole camp gathered round to watch.

The salesman ran the drill
down one track.
John Henry began pounding
his 14-pound hammers down another.

Well, they went at it all morning.
The steam-powered drill
hissed and whined like a caged animal.
John Henry was quieter.
He whistled softly
in rhythm with his blows.
But the sweat washing down his back
made little rivers in the dirt.

Soon the dust rose up
as thick as a deep fog.
It was hard to see clearly.
But everyone could still hear
the cold steel of John Henry's hammers
and the whirring of the steam drill.
At noon, the contest ended.

The dust settled.

All holes were measured.

The steam drill had dug three holes,
as round and clean as you please.

But John Henry looked back over five holes
of his own.

That made him the winner.

John Henry raised his arms in victory.

His fellow workers stomped and cheered.

But the price of winning was high.

Even before the last cheers passed away,

John staggered on his feet.

The crowd grew suddenly quiet.

John took one more step.

Then he fell to the ground,

his hammers still gripped tight.

The foreman rushed right up.

But there was nothing anyone could do.

John Henry was gone.

The machine couldn't beat him,

but it had cost him his life.

The Big Bend Tunnel has long been done.
And the trains passing through it
don't mark the spot where John Henry fell.
But some folks say
that if you listen hard at either end,
you can still hear his hammers
pounding away in the dark.